SEAHORSES

Darla Duhaime

Rourke
Educational Media

rourkeeducationalmedia.com

Before & After Reading Activities

Teaching Focus:
Concepts of Print- Have students find capital letters and punctuation in a sentence. Ask students to explain the purpose for using them in a sentence.

Before Reading:

Building Academic Vocabulary and Background Knowledge
Before reading a book, it is important to set the stage for your child or student by using pre-reading strategies. This will help them develop their vocabulary, increase their reading comprehension, and make connections across the curriculum.
1. *Read the title and look at the cover. Let's make predictions about what this book will be about.*
2. *Take a picture walk by talking about the pictures/photographs in the book. Implant the vocabulary as you take the picture walk. Be sure to talk about the text features such as headings, Table of Contents, glossary, bolded words, captions, charts/ diagrams, or Index.*
3. Have students read the first page of text with you then have students read the remaining text.
4. *Strategy Talk – use to assist students while reading.*
   - *Get your mouth ready*
   - *Look at the picture*
   - *Think…does it make sense*
   - *Think…does it look right*
   - *Think…does it sound right*
   - *Chunk it – by looking for a part you know*
5. *Read it again.*

Content Area Vocabulary
Use glossary words in a sentence.

environment
mate
predators
ridges

After Reading:

Comprehension and Extension Activity
After reading the book, work on the following questions with your child or students in order to check their level of reading comprehension and content mastery.
1. *What do seahorses use their tails for? (Summarize)*
2. *What do seahorses eat? (Asking Questions)*
3. *How are seahorses different from people? (Text to Self Connection)*
4. *How do seahorses travel long distances? (Asking Questions)*

Extension Activity
Draw a picture of a seahorse family in their ocean home. Label the mom and the dad. Don't forget to draw lots of baby seahorses!

Table of Contents

Seahorse Tails

Seahorses live near the ocean floor. Like most fish, they have tails. But seahorses don't use their tails to swim!

Seahorses use their tails to hold onto seagrass and coral. They use their snouts to suck tiny floating animals from the water. Seahorses eat all day long!

snout

Slow Swimmers

Seahorses are slow swimmers. They have a small fin on their backs. It can flutter 35 times per second.

fin

Seahorses use their tails to hitch a ride with floating seaweed. This lets them travel long distances without swimming!

A seahorse's body is covered in bony **ridges**. It can change color to blend in with its **environment**.

ridges

Seahorses can move their eyes in opposite directions. They can look for food with one eye and **predators** with the other.

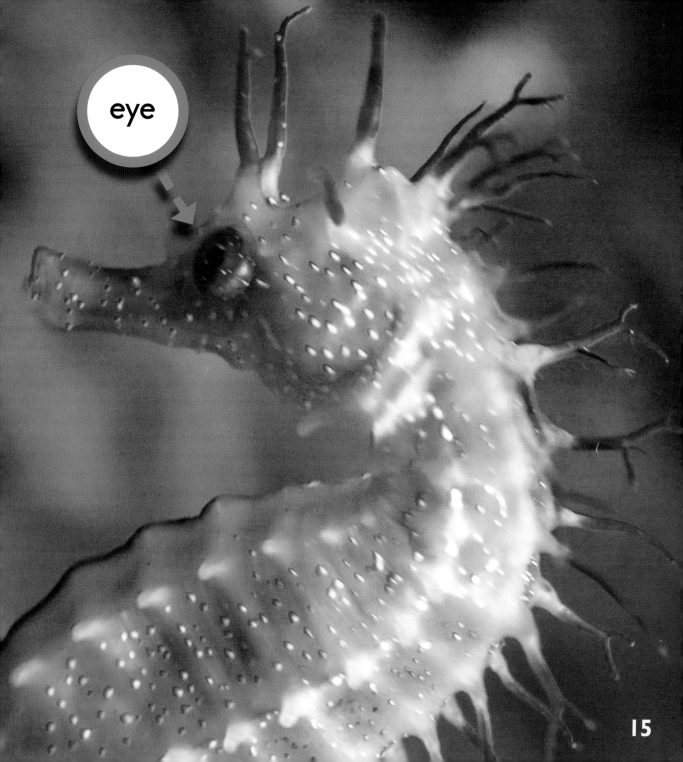

eye

15

Life Partners

Seahorses **mate** for life. The couple meets every morning. They link their tails and swim together.

Male seahorses have a pouch like a kangaroo. The female puts eggs in her mate's pouch. He can have 2,000 babies at a time!

pouch

Seahorses are noisy! They make growling and clicking noises.

Fun Facts

There are 47 kinds of seahorses.

A baby seahorse is called a fry.

A group of seahorses is called a herd.

A seahorse has no teeth and no stomach.

A young seahorse eats about 3,000 pieces of food a day.

Picture Glossary

 **environment** (en-VYE-ruhn-muhnt): The natural surroundings of living things.

 **mate** (mate): Join together to produce babies.

 **predators** (PRED-uh-turs): Animals that hunt other animals for food.

 **ridges** (rij-iz): Narrow, raised strips on the outside of something.

Index

Websites to Visit

www.nationalgeographic.com/animals/fish/hub/seahorses

www.theseahorsetrust.org/seahorse-facts.aspx

www.nwf.org/Kids/Ranger-Rick/Animals/Fish/Seahorses.aspx

Meet The Author!
www.meetREMauthors.com

About the Author

Darla Duhaime is fascinated by sea creatures and their amazing ocean habitats. When she is not writing books for kids, you can often find her gazing at the ocean, dreaming up new stories.

www.rourkeeducationalmedia.com

PHOTO CREDITS: Cover and title page ©Frolova_Elena; p.5 ©Kjeld Friis; p.7 ©urf; p.9 ©JillianSuzanne; p.10-11 ©Rich Carey; p.13, 23 ©JenniMaijaHelena; p.15, 23 ©wrangel; p.17, 23 ©Markus Schieder; p.19 ©Nature Picture Library/Alamy Stock Photo; p.21 ©feathercollector; p.23 ©Frhojdysz | Dreamstime.com (predator)

Edited by: Keli Sipperley
Cover and Interior design by: Rhea Magaro-Wallace

Library of Congress PCN Data

Seahorses / Darla Duhaime
(Ocean Animals)
ISBN (hard cover)(alk. paper) 978-1-68342-328-7
ISBN (soft cover) 978-1-68342-424-6
ISBN (e-Book) 978-1-68342-494-9
Library of Congress Control Number: 2017931175

Printed in the United States of America, North Mankato, Minnesota